BioDetectives: Investigations in Forensics

Biology

PEARSON

Prentice
Hall

Boston, Massachusetts
Upper Saddle River, New Jersey

To the Teacher

BioDetectives: Investigations in Forensics contains investigations in forensic science that are closely related to the topics in each unit of the *Prentice Hall Biology* textbook. Each investigation is preceded by background information to help students complete the investigation.

The BioDetectives Videotapes that accompany the *BioDetectives: Investigations in Forensics* depict activities that are not appropriate for the student laboratory (field observations and the study of human pathogens). The topics on the video segments are not related to the activities in this book. However, page 63 in this book provides answers to the questions raised on the videotapes.

ISBN 0-13-115289-0

7 8 9 10   11 10 09 08 07

Contents

BioDetectives Videotapes: Summaries of Video Segments

Videotape 1

- **UNIT 1 History's Mystery: An Introduction to Forensic Science** Modern forensic scientists reenact a historical crime to show how scientific clues can be used to identify the criminal.
- **UNIT 2 *Pfiesteria*: A Killer in the Water** Scientists work to discover the cause of mysterious sores on swimmers' skin and the deaths of thousands of fish in a river in North Carolina.

Videotape 2

- **UNIT 3 Skin Cancer: Deadly Cells** Treating melanoma requires understanding the basic biology of many kinds of cells. Scientists with a new idea about how to destroy cancer cells form a hypothesis and perform an experiment to test it.
- **UNIT 4 Coming Home: A Nation's Pledge** Scientists use the mitochondrial DNA in bone fragments to identify the remains of soldiers reported missing in action in Vietnam.
- **UNIT 5 The Galápagos Islands: A Glimpse Into the Past** These islands are a hotbed of research for the study of evolution. Fossils in ancient lava tubes help to test an unusual theory about the history of life in the Galápagos.
- **UNIT 5 Mummies: Ties to the Past** Ninety-six preserved mummies are discovered in South America and are used to gain insight into the lives of the world's first mummy-makers.
- **UNIT 6 Hantavirus: A Tale of Mice and People** Scientists use field observations and laboratory experiments to solve the puzzle of how a strange, deadly illness is caused and transmitted. In the process, they discover a surprising explanation for an old Native American health practice.

Videotape 3

- **UNIT 8 Insect Clues: The Smallest Witnesses** One of the most important clues to solving crimes is figuring out when the crime occurred. Forensic scientists use experiments and field observations to understand the natural process of decomposition.
- **UNIT 9 Wrongly Accused: Science and Justice** Forensic scientists use modern DNA-based techniques to challenge a conviction based on an older technique—identification of suspects from hair samples.
- **UNIT 10 Influenza: Tracking a Virus** Scientists analyze DNA in decades-old tissue samples to try to solve the mystery of the origin of the deadly strain of virus that was responsible for the worldwide 1918 influenza epidemic.

Using Polarized Light to Identify Fibers

Background

Whenever two objects come into contact, dust is usually transferred between them. This dust can include hairs and clothing fibers. Scientists often use dust as evidence of whether a suspect was involved in a crime. Evidence is anything that is used to help determine the truth. A person who uses scientific knowledge to help answer legal questions, such as in the investigation of a crime, is called a forensic scientist. A forensic scientist can, for example, compare a suspect's hair with a hair found at a crime scene. A match between these samples may indicate that the suspect was present at the scene.

Identifying dust particles requires careful handling and knowledge of their structure. At a crime scene, pieces of evidence are individually wrapped in paper or are put inside plastic collection bags. These papers and bags are then taken to a forensic laboratory that is kept as dust-free as possible. There, forensic scientists unwrap each paper or bag and place each item separately on clean paper. They examine the evidence, first with the unaided eye and then with a dissecting microscope, making drawings and photographs of their observations. Next, the scientists use transparent tape to transfer the dust samples to microscope slides for more detailed examination.

One of the most valuable techniques for making the details of microscopic specimens visible is the use of polarized light. To understand how this technique can make for better viewing, you must first understand what polarized light is.

Imagine standing in the dark and watching the headlight of a motorcycle from the side as it travels up and down a series of small hills. This up and down motion of the headlight, shown in Figure 1A, is similar to the shape of light waves.

Now suppose you are looking at the motorcycle headlight as it approaches you. You would then see the headlight moving up and down. This up-and-down direction

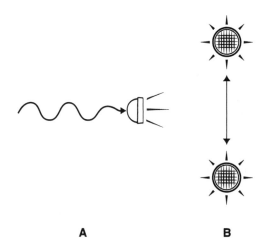

A The path of the motorcycle headlight seen from the side as it goes over hills. **B** The motorcycle headlight seen from the front as it vibrates in only one direction, like polarized light waves.

FIGURE 1

of a light wave is called the vibrational direction, as shown in Figure 1B. Light that consists of waves that all have the same vibrational direction is said to be polarized. Light that consists of waves with different vibrational directions is said to be unpolarized.

Most light is unpolarized. Light can be made polarized by passing it through a polarizing filter. A polarizing filter, as shown in Figure 2A on the next page, is made up of many long, parallel molecules. Just as a piece of paper can pass through a comb only if it is parallel to the comb's teeth, only those light waves that vibrate in parallel with these molecules can pass through the filter.

What if light waves pass through two polarizing filters whose molecules are parallel to each other, as shown in Figure 2B? The second filter does not block any light waves that the first filter has not already blocked. Thus, the second filter has no effect on the light. But suppose one of the filters is rotated, as shown in Figure 2C, so that its

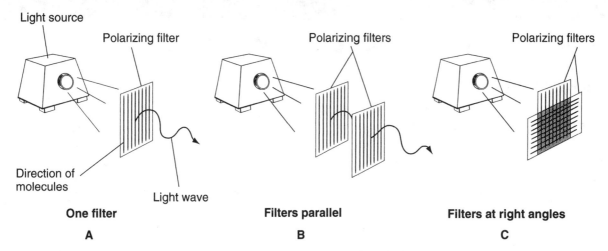

Light source

Polarizing filter

Direction of molecules

Light wave

One filter

A

Polarizing filters

Filters parallel

B

Polarizing filters

Filters at right angles

C

Transmission of light through polarizing filters. **A** One polarizing filter blocks most light, and allows light waves that vibrate in parallel with the filter's molecules to pass through the filter. **B** Adding a second filter parallel to the first has no effect. **C** Rotating the second filter so that its molecules are at right angles to the molecules in the first filter blocks nearly all the light.

FIGURE 2

molecules are at right angles to the molecules of the other filter. Then, all of the light waves will be blocked.

Hair and some other types of fibers that are made of long, parallel molecules can act like polarizing filters. However, when light with a vibrational direction that is not parallel with the hair's molecules passes through the hair, the hair does not simply block the light. Instead, the hair changes the light's vibrational direction. Recall that white light is a mixture of light of different colors. The change in a light wave's vibrational direction depends on its color.

When polarized white light passes through a hair that is being viewed under a microscope, the light comes through the hair as a mixture of many colors. Each color has a different vibrational direction. If a forensic scientist places a polarizing filter on top of the eyepiece of the

microscope, it will block most of the light coming through the microscope. This polarizing filter is called an analyzer.

As the forensic scientist rotates the analyzer, one color at a time becomes visible. The forensic scientist sees a pattern of color on the edges of the hair that changes as the analyzer is rotated. Similar color patterns appear when similar fibers are examined. The scientist must record which position of the analyzer causes each color to appear.

As these color changes occur, pairs of black lines can also appear along the hairs. These lines are areas where parallel molecules in the hair have completely blocked all the light. As the analyzer is rotated, these lines appear to move. The rotation of the analyzer is the same for similar hair samples. This effect gives the scientist another way to compare hairs from known and unknown sources.

Using Polarized Light to Identify Fibers

Investigation

CASE SUMMARY

Detectives have retrieved several fiber samples from both the scene of a crime and a suspect's home. They believe that matching these samples will give them information to help solve the crime. You have been asked to examine the fibers to determine whether any of them match one another. You will have to draw conclusions from your observations and report them in court.

QUESTION FOR FORENSIC ANALYSIS

Can microscopic examination provide a match of fiber samples taken from the scene of a crime with those taken from the suspect's home?

MATERIALS (*per group*)

microscope   unlined paper

8 microscope slides   polarizing filter

coverslips   dissecting probe

dropper pipette   forceps

7 fiber samples   analyzer

SAFETY

Be careful with sharp dissecting probes and with glass microscope slides and coverslips, which can break and cut you.

PROCEDURE

1. Place a microscope slide on a polarizing filter. **CAUTION:** *Microscope slides can break and cut you.*

2. Use a dissecting probe and forceps to remove a strand of fiber from one of the known samples. **CAUTION:** *Dissecting probes are sharp.*

3. Use the dropper pipette to place a drop of water on the microscope slide. Position the strand of fiber in the water and add a coverslip. **CAUTION:** *Glass coverslips are easily broken and can cut you.*

4. Mount the slide and polarizing filter on the stage of the microscope. Then, adjust and focus the microscope.

5. Place the analyzer on top of the microscope's eyepiece with the white mark facing toward you. Look through the analyzer. The field of view should be dark.

6. Rotate the analyzer until the image is sharpest. In the Data Table, record the position of the analyzer (the number of degrees you turned the analyzer clockwise or counterclockwise to obtain this image).

Name_____ Class_____ Date _____

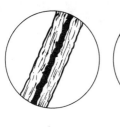
A
Human hair

B
Animal hair

C
Animal hair

D
Synthetic Fiber

E
Twisted Fiber

FIGURE 3

7. On a separate sheet of paper, sketch and label the image, using Figure 3 as a guide. On your sketch, record the position of any colored areas that you observed.

8. In the Data Table, record the position of the analyzer for each color change you observed.

9. Repeat steps 1 through 8 for each sample. If you need more space to record your observations, continue the Data Table on a separate sheet of paper.

DATA TABLE

Sample	Position of Analyzer (degrees clockwise or counterclockwise)	Color

10. Compare your sketches and record any matches you find between the unknown samples and the known samples.

ANALYSIS AND CONCLUSIONS

1. **Comparing and Contrasting** Did any of the unknown samples match any of the known samples? Consider the shape, texture, and behavior in polarized light of each sample in your answer. List any matches that you identified with an explanation of the evidence you relied on to determine each match.

_____

_____

_____

_____

_____

_____

2. **Analyzing Data** Were the differences among samples clear enough to determine whether any of the unknown samples were the same as any of the known samples? Explain your answer.

_____

_____

_____

_____

3. **Inferring** From your observations, can you conclude whether the suspect is responsible for the crime? Explain your answer.

_____

_____

_____

_____

4. **Communicating Results** Write a paragraph summarizing your conclusions in a way that you could present in a courtroom. Be sure to include your sketches.

_____

_____

_____

_____

_____

_____

Using Range and Habitat to Track Evidence

Background

Many organisms are found only in certain regions or habitats. Therefore, the presence of these organisms in smuggled or illegal goods can help reveal the source of the goods. If a forensic scientist found camel hairs on evidence, the scientist could suspect that the evidence had been in north Africa or southwest Asia, where camels are common. Likewise, the scientist could conclude that the evidence had been in one of the deserts of that region, a habitat where camels are well adapted to survive. This conclusion is based on the fact that the distribution of camels is limited in two ways: Their range consists largely of one geographic region (north Africa and southwest Asia), and they live largely in one kind of habitat (deserts).

The distribution of many species is limited in both these ways. One such species found only in a specific range and habitat is the caterpillar fungus. A fungus is a eukaryotic heterotroph with cell walls. Fungi survive as decomposers or, in some cases, as parasites. Most species of fungi require a moist environment and reproduce by releasing spores, or dormant reproductive cells.

The caterpillar fungus (*Cordyceps sinensis)*, found mostly in south central China, is a parasite of the caterpillars of a certain species of moth. When a caterpillar inhales spores of this fungus through its breathing pores, the spores sprout inside the caterpillar, producing a mass of threadlike fungal cells called hyphae. Figure 1 shows the typical appearance of hyphae. As the fungus grows, it digests the caterpillar from the inside and produces a reproductive structure

called a fruiting body, shown in Figure 1. Wind spreads the spores that form inside the fruiting body to the next generation of caterpillars.

Like most fungi, the caterpillar fungus requires a moist environment. It is common in marshy grasslands and at high altitudes, where the climate conditions and presence of prey caterpillars permit it to live. Thus, like camels, the caterpillar fungus has both a limited geographic range (south central China) and a limited habitat (marshy grasslands and high altitudes). If the caterpillar fungus is found in evidence, its narrow range and habitat would make it useful to forensic scientists as an indicator of where the evidence has been.

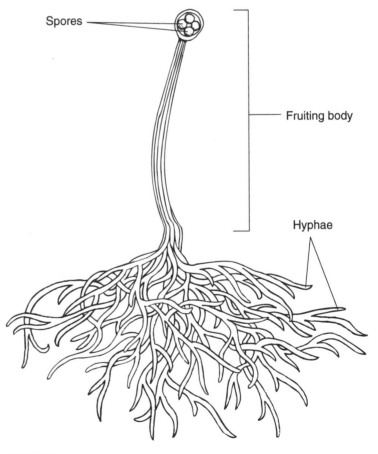

Spores

Fruiting body

Hyphae

FIGURE 1

Using Range and Habitat to Track Evidence

Investigation

CASE SUMMARY

Customs inspectors opened a suspicious package of food products that was being imported from Australia. They found several stolen diamonds hidden in a box of cookies. The shipment had been stored in a warm, moist environment that enabled fungi to grow on some of the food products, including the cookies among which the diamonds were hidden. The police suspected that the shipment had been packed elsewhere before being sent through Australia to the United States in order to conceal its source. Australian customs officials opened some of the boxes in the shipment but did not find the diamonds. You are asked to use the information collected about the fungi found on the cookies to determine where the shipment was packed.

QUESTION FOR FORENSIC ANALYSIS

Where were the diamonds and food products packed?

MATERIALS (per group)

7 different colored pencils

PROCEDURE

1. The following species of fungi were found in the cookies that the United States customs inspectors confiscated:

   Amanita muscara

   Aseroe rubra

   Nyctalis mirabilis

   Tubaria rufofulva

   Hygrophorus lewellinae

   Microporus xanthopus

   Hyphodontiella multiseptata

   Use the information in Figure 2 on page 14 to draw the borders of the range of *Amanita muscara* on the map in Figure 3 on page 15 with a colored pencil. Label the range you have drawn with the name of the species.

2. Using a different colored pencil for each species, repeat step 1 with each of the species found in the evidence.

Species	Range	Habitat	Appearance	Additional Information
Amanita muscara	Southeast Australia	In forests under pine trees	Mushroom with red spotted cap and white stalk	Forms symbiotic associations (mycorrhizae) with many plants
Aseroe rubra	Southeast Australia	In open forests and mountain grasslands	Mushroom with white stalk; cap has bright red arms	Has a strong odor of rotten meat
Nyctalis mirabilis	Southeast Australia	In cool, temperate rainforests	Mushroom with silver-grey cap and white stalk	Grows on old mushrooms of other species
Cordyceps sinensis	South-central China	In cold marshes and under trees above 4000 m.	Spikelike fruiting body on dead caterpillars	Is a parasite of caterpillars of the moth *Hepilus fabricius*
Tubaria rufofulva	Throughout southeast Asia	In soil and decaying wood	Red mushroom	Grows on wood
Hygrophorus lewellinae	Coastal areas of Indonesia	Grows among low plants along stream banks	White mushroom with waxy cap	Is common on ferns
Microporus xanthopus	Laos, Sumatra, and Borneo	Grows symbiotically with algae as a lichen on termite nests	Forms a shelf with many small pores, attached to a yellow disk-shaped base	Grows attached to trees
Hyphodontiella multiseptata	Sumatra and Borneo	On tree trunks and termite nests	Grows in a flat sheet	Grows symbiotically with algae as a lichen

FIGURE 2

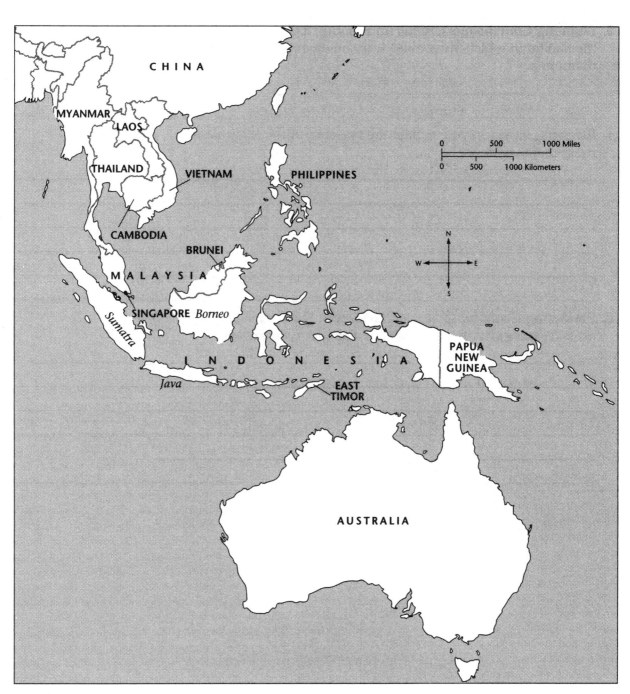

FIGURE 3

ANALYSIS AND CONCLUSIONS

1. **Analyzing Data** According to your map, where do all of the species of fungi found in the cookies occur?

_____

2. **Drawing Conclusions** Where can you conclude that the shipment of diamonds was packed?

_____

3. **Drawing Conclusions** Use the information in Figure 2 to describe the habitat in which the cookies were made or packed with the diamonds.

_____

_____

4. **Inferring** How can you explain the presence of the Australian fungi in the evidence?

_____

_____

_____

_____

_____

_____

5. **Predicting** Could fungi be used to identify the source of stolen artifacts smuggled from the Sahara? Explain your answer.

_____

_____

_____

_____

_____

_____

Using Tissues as Evidence

Background

Histology is the study of the structure of tissues. A tissue is a group of specialized cells that work together to perform a specific function in an organism. This area of biology is especially important in pathology, the study of diseases. Scientists who study the differences between healthy and diseased tissues are called histopathologists. Their research is used by physicians to identify diseases and to determine how serious a patient's condition is.

The work of a histopathologist is critical in identifying and treating cancer. By examining a tissue sample under the microscope, a histopathologist can help determine whether a cancer is present. If a cancer is found, a histopathologist can identify the type of cancer. This information is extremely important in deciding how to treat the cancer.

Histological evidence is often important in lawsuits that claim a consumer product or other substance caused a person to become ill or die. This has happened in several lawsuits that people have filed against tobacco companies for causing their lung cancer. Tobacco is not the only cause of lung cancer. There are several other factors that make lung cancer likely, including the inheritance of cancer-promoting forms of certain genes and the inhaling of materials such as asbestos. However, the types of lung damage and cancer that smokers develop are different from those that occur in people whose lungs were damaged in some other way. Thus, the testimony of a histopathologist who can recognize these differences is often one of the most important parts of a smoker's lawsuit.

A smoker's lungs are usually damaged in other ways before cancer develops. Figure 1 shows the typical pattern of damage to a smoker's lungs. Tobacco smoke destroys the cells that line the breathing passages. These cells have small hairlike extensions called cilia that normally sweep mucus and particles of smoke and dust out and away from the lungs. Without these cells, mucus and smoke particles accumulate in the breathing passages, causing what is known as "smoker's cough." At the same time, new mucus glands form and secrete more mucus into the already-blocked breathing passages. This blockage can interfere with breathing and can cause part of the lungs to collapse.

A

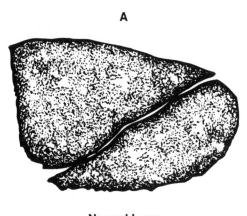

Normal Lung

B

Collapsed lung tissue   Smoke debris

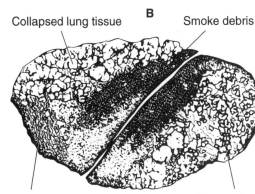

Solid cancer tissue   Fibrous tissue

Smoker's Lung

FIGURE 1

Two other lung problems that often occur before cancer develops are bronchitis and emphysema. Bronchitis is the inflammation of the bronchi, the tubes that carry air in and out of the lungs. Emphysema is a disease of the alveoli, the microscopic air sacs that make up most of the lungs. The thin tissues of the alveoli are only one cell thick, but they have an enormous surface area. This surface is where oxygen passes from inhaled air into the bloodstream, as well as where carbon dioxide is released from the bloodstream into exhaled air. In emphysema, the alveoli break down and fuse, forming large open spaces. This process reduces the surface area available for gas exchange, and the patient becomes weakened by a lack of oxygen. The lung loses elasticity, which makes breathing more difficult.

Eventually, the person with emphysema may develop lung cancer.

The type and location of cancers caused by smoking are different from those of other types of lung cancer. Many smokers develop cancer in the bronchi or the bronchioles, the smaller branches of the bronchi. Cancers in these locations are rare in nonsmokers. A histopathologist can often identify the type of lung cell that became cancerous.

Smokers tend to develop cancer in different types of cells than do nonsmokers. A type of cancer called small cell carcinoma is common in smokers, while rare in nonsmokers. Small cell carcinoma often begins in the bronchi and grows in cords or small, grapelike clusters. Under the microscope, the cancer appears darker than the surrounding tissue. The type and location of the cancer are important facts in a histopathologist's testimony in a smoking-related lawsuit.

Using Tissues as Evidence

Investigation

CASE SUMMARY

A smoker is suing a tobacco company for causing his cancer. The company is trying to argue that, in this case, the patient's cancer was not caused by smoking. You have been asked to compare lung tissue from the patient to cancerous and healthy lung tissues and report your observations and conclusions to the court.

QUESTION FOR FORENSIC ANALYSIS

Does the patient have the typical signs of tissue damage and cancer due to smoking?

SAFETY

Always carry the microscope with two hands.
Handle glass slides with care to avoid breakage.

MATERIALS (*per group*)

compound microscope
prepared slide of normal human lung tissue
prepared slide of smoker's cancerous lung tissue
prepared slide of patient's lung tissue

PROCEDURE

1. View the prepared slide of normal human lung tissue with the microscope at low magnification and then at high magnification. Draw and label your observations of the slide in the appropriate field-of-view circle in Figure 2 and record the magnification.
2. Repeat Step 1 with each of the other prepared slides.
3. Label any parts of your drawings that indicate similarities or differences between the patient's lung tissue and either of the other two slides. Use the additional space provided in Figure 2 to draw and label details of the similarities and differences that you observed.

ANALYSIS AND CONCLUSIONS

1. **Comparing and Contrasting** What differences did you observe between the normal and cancerous lung tissues?

   _____

   _____

   _____

Name_____ Class_____ Date _____

Magnification _____ Magnification _____ Magnification _____
Normal human lung tissue Cancerous human lung tissue Patient's lung tissue

Additional observations:

FIGURE 2

2. **Analyzing Data** Did you see evidence of other diseases in the cancerous lung tissue? Explain your answer.

_____

_____

_____

3. **Drawing Conclusions** Did the patient's lung tissue more closely resemble the normal tissue or the cancerous tissue? Explain your answer.

_____

_____

_____

4. **Evaluating** Are you confident that the patient's cancer was caused by smoking? State the reasons for your answer.

_____

_____

_____

5. **Inferring** How would you expect the growth of a solid cancer mass in the lungs to affect a smoker's ability to obtain oxygen? Explain your answer.

_____

_____

_____

Name_____ Class_____ Date _____

Interpreting DNA Analysis

Background

One of the most useful tools in forensic science is a technique for identifying small quantities of DNA, which may be found as part of the evidence used in a criminal trial. This technique is called polymerase chain reaction, or PCR. PCR enables forensic scientists to make millions of copies of DNA molecules so that the scientists can analyze the DNA by using gel electrophoresis. Gel electrophoresis is a process that uses an electric field to sort DNA molecules by size.

Base sequences of DNA vary widely among people. Because of this, forensic scientists can use PCR and gel electrophoresis to identify an individual from a small amount of DNA left behind on an object such as a drinking glass.

DNA polymerase, the enzyme that gives PCR its name, is found in all living things and is important in the synthesis of DNA. This enzyme catalyzes the formation of a complementary strand for single-stranded DNA. As shown in Figure 1, DNA polymerase does this by attaching additional nucleotides to the end of an existing double-stranded region of DNA. However, because DNA polymerase cannot begin the formation of the complementary strand, a short

fragment of complementary DNA must be in place before this enzyme can act.

Figure 2 on page 22 shows the steps involved in PCR. First, a sample of DNA is placed in a solution containing nucleotides, DNA polymerase, and one or more short pieces of single-stranded DNA, called primers. This mixture is heated to break the bonds between the two DNA strands. These strands then separate, as shown in Figure 2A.

Next, the mixture is cooled, which allows the primers to attach to the separated strands wherever there is a complementary sequence, as in Figure 2B. As a primer attaches to the strands, that region of DNA becomes double-stranded. DNA polymerase then binds to these double-stranded regions and continues to add nucleotides beside the primers. This action extends the double-stranded regions until they reach the end of the DNA molecule or a special stop sequence in the DNA. Notice in Figure 2B that this process works simultaneously in opposite directions on the two strands.

At this point, each original DNA molecule in the sample has become *two* DNA molecules. The next step is to repeat the entire process. Figure 2C shows how

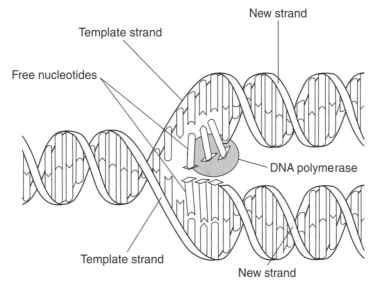

FIGURE 1

this is done. The mixture is heated again to separate the DNA strands. Primers attach to the DNA, giving DNA polymerase a new starting place. DNA polymerase once again assembles complementary strands. By the end of this step, each original DNA molecule has become *four* molecules.

This cycle of heating and cooling can be repeated until the quantity of DNA has increased enough to be visible on an electrophoresis gel. Twenty PCR cycles can increase the number of DNA molecules in a sample one millionfold.

In addition, notice that each of the primers in Figure 2B starts in a different

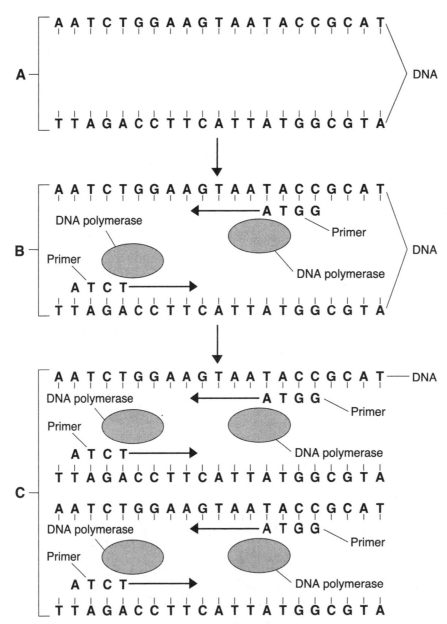

The PCR technique **A** The mixture is heated until the DNA strands separate. **B** The mixture is cooled. Primers and DNA polymerase attach to the sample DNA. DNA polymerase adds nucleotides to the primers, extending the double-stranded regions in the direction of the arrows. **C** The mixture is heated and cooled again. The DNA strands separate, primers and DNA polymerase attach again to DNA, and DNA polymerase builds new matching strands for each single-stranded DNA molecule.

FIGURE 2

place on the DNA strands. As a result, the newly formed DNA molecules are not all the same length. The strands made with the primer with the sequence ATGG start in farther and are shorter. Those made with the primer ATCT are longer. As a result, half the DNA strands produced in the PCR procedure will be of the shorter type, whereas the other half will be of the longer type. If more than two primers are used, the DNA strands that are produced will have varying lengths.

These differences in length are important because they enable forensic scientists to separate the DNA strands by gel electrophoresis. Because each person's DNA is unique, PCR will produce a unique pattern of DNA fragments for each person. Gel electrophoresis can be used to compare the patterns in DNA from several sources. Examine Figure 3, which is a diagram of an electrophoresis gel. It has seven lanes, marked with the letters A through G. DNA samples have been placed in each rectangular well at the top of the gel. The DNA samples move down the gel from these wells. Because smaller DNA molecules move faster than larger ones, the molecules sort themselves out by size into the bands that you see in each lane.

The samples placed in lanes A and G were identical mixtures of DNA molecules, and the sizes of those DNA molecules are known. Thus, each band in these lanes can be labeled with the size of the DNA molecules it contains. The forensic scientist can then determine the sizes of the DNA molecules in the bands in all the other lanes by comparing their positions to those of the known bands in lanes A and G. These measurements are recorded in units of thousands of bases, or kilobases. Similarities and differences in the sizes of DNA molecules can be used to link evidence such as bloodstains and hair to specific individuals.

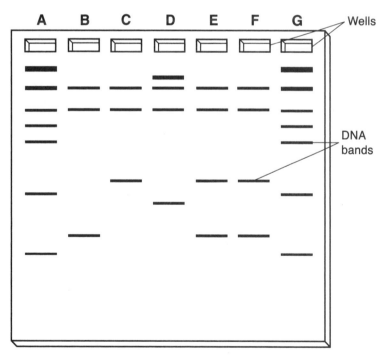

Diagram of an electrophoresis gel Letters A through G mark the lanes in which the DNA spreads out from the wells. Bands at the bottom contain the shortest DNA molecules.

FIGURE 3

Interpreting DNA Analysis

Investigation

CASE SUMMARY

You are a forensic scientist who specializes in the analysis of DNA. The police have brought you four samples of evidence. The first is a blood sample from the victim of a crime. The second is a blood sample from a suspect who claims to have been elsewhere when the crime occurred. The third sample was collected at the crime scene, and the fourth sample was taken from the suspect's shoe. You are asked to compare the DNA in these samples to determine whether there is sufficient evidence to connect the suspect with the crime scene or with the victim.

QUESTION FOR FORENSIC ANALYSIS

Does the analysis of DNA from the evidence gathered at the crime scene connect the suspect with the crime scene?

PROCEDURE

1. Examine Figure 3 on page 23, and locate lanes A and G. Starting with the wells below letters A and G, compare the patterns of DNA bands in these two lanes.

2. Then, examine lanes B through F. Compare their patterns of DNA bands.

3. Recall that wells A and G contained a standard mixture of DNA. Starting at the top and moving down, the lengths of the DNA molecules in this mixture, in kilobases, are:

   5.0, 4.1, 3.5, 3.1, 2.8, 1.9, and 0.7.

   Keep in mind that the smaller the molecules of DNA, the farther they move down through the gel. In lanes A and G, label each band with the length of the DNA molecules it contains.

4. Using the lengths of the DNA molecules in lanes A and G as your standards, estimate the lengths of the DNA molecules in lanes B through F. In Figure 3, label each band with the estimated length of the DNA molecules it contains.

5. Based on your findings in Step 4, which samples appear to be identical? Record this information in the Data Table.

DATA TABLE

Lane	Source of DNA Sample	Identical Lanes
B	Victim of the crime	
C	Suspect	
D	Person unrelated to the crime	
E	Evidence found at crime scene	
F	Suspect's shoe	

ANALYSIS AND CONCLUSIONS

1. **Measuring** Which sample(s) contained DNA molecules that were approximately 1 kilobase long? Approximately 2 kilobases long?

   _____

   _____

   _____

2. **Controlling Variables** Why were the samples in lanes A and G necessary?

   _____

   _____

   _____

   _____

3. **Analyzing Data** What can you conclude about the suspect's presence at the crime scene from the bands estimated to be at approximately 4 kilobases and approximately 3.5 kilobases in lanes B through F?

   _____

   _____

   _____

   _____

   _____

4. **Inferring** Based on your findings, was the suspect present at the crime scene? Explain your answer.

   _____

   _____

   _____

   _____

Identifying Feathers

Background

Wildlife forensics involves the investigation of crimes against wildlife resources, such as the hunting of endangered species. Much of the work of a forensic wildlife scientist consists of identifying the species from which various products were made. This task is often difficult because scientists who first receive the evidence may not be familiar with species that live in other parts of the world. As a result, they are not always able to recognize materials that were taken from endangered species.

When forensic scientists in the field are in doubt about wildlife products that they receive, they can send them to specialists at one of the laboratories of the United States Fish and Wildlife Service for identification. Among the scientists at those laboratories are experts in the classification of birds, fish, and other groups of animals. These specialists identify the species of wildlife products and examine the evidence for links between a suspect, an animal victim, and a crime scene.

The evidence that wildlife forensic scientists examine often includes handicrafts, jewelry, or clothing made with feathers. The scientists must identify the feathers used in these products to ensure that they were not taken from an endangered species. One of the first steps in identifying a feather is determining what type it is. There are two main types of feathers—down and contour feathers. Down feathers are found on young birds and underneath the contour feathers of some adult birds. As shown in Figure 1A, a down feather has a short, hollow central shaft called a rachis. The rachis has many long, flexible branches known as barbs, and each barb has many small side branches called barbules. The long, flexible barbs of a down feather form a loose, soft "puff."

A contour feather, which is shown in Figure 1B, is the large, flat feather that covers most of an adult bird's body. Notice that these feathers have a longer, thicker rachis than down feathers do. Their barbules are held together by tiny hooks, or barbicels, to form the flat part of the feather called the vane. At the base of the feather is a fluffy, or plumulaceous, portion.

When wildlife forensic scientists in the United States examine a feather, they always look to see whether it was taken from a bald eagle. The bald eagle is protected by law as an endangered species. Possession of bald eagle feathers without a special permit is

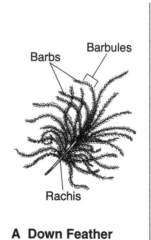

A Down Feather

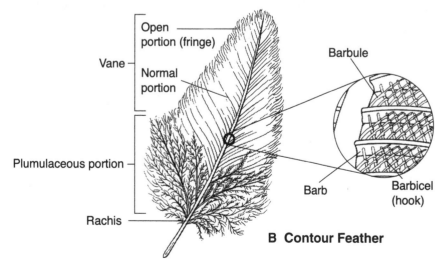

B Contour Feather

FIGURE 1

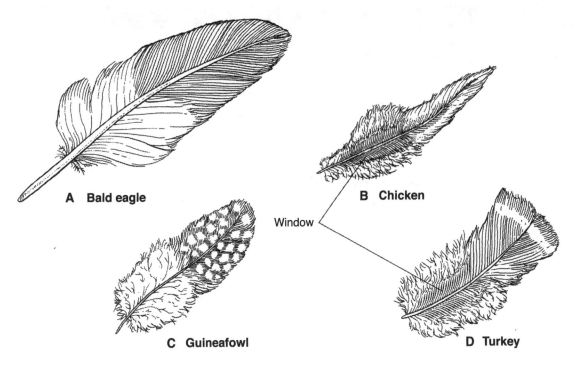

A **Bald eagle**

B **Chicken**

C **Guineafowl**

D **Turkey**

Window

FIGURE 2

illegal. Figure 2A on page 28 shows a typical contour feather of a bald eagle. This feather has a white base, with the top two thirds of the feather dark brown or black. The border between the two colors often forms an uneven V shape.

Usually, the feathers used in crafts come from domesticated birds such as chickens, turkeys, and guineafowl, shown in Figures 2B to 2D. In chickens, contour feathers are flexible and taper to a point. A V-shaped fringe covers the edge of the vane. Chicken feathers can be white, black, brown, or green in color; the fringe may be a different color from the rest of the vane. Turkey feathers have a square tip with a very short fringe. They may be white or brown with slender black bars. In both chicken and turkey feathers, the bases of the barbs in the plumulaceous portion lie parallel near the rachis. They form a narrow, flat strip called a "window," as shown in Figure 2B and D. By contrast, guineafowl contour feathers have a vane with a rounded tip and light spots on a black background; smaller speckles may surround the spots. Also, the plumulaceous portion is gray and dense. The feathers of domesticated birds are often dyed when they are used in crafts, but they are easy to identify even after dyeing.

Identifying Feathers

Investigation

CASE SUMMARY

A customs official in Great Britain recently confiscated a shipment of Native American jewelry and clothing. The official suspected that some of the goods were decorated with bald eagle feathers, which cannot be exported for sale. The British customs service has forwarded these materials to you for identification. You are asked to determine whether the feathers came from a common domesticated bird or a bald eagle. The British custom service will use your report in deciding whether to return the goods to the owner or to charge the owner with importing illegal items.

QUESTION FOR FORENSIC ANALYSIS

Did the feather taken as evidence come from a bald eagle or from a common domesticated bird?

MATERIALS (per group)

hand lens
down feather from a domesticated bird
contour feather from a domesticated bird
plastic gloves
feather taken as evidence

PROCEDURE

1. After putting on plastic gloves, closely examine the contour feather with a hand lens. Locate the rachis, barbs, and barbules. Draw and label your observations in the space provided in Figure 3.
2. Gently ruffle the edge of the contour feather with your finger and observe the effect on the vane. Smooth the feather with your finger and notice how easily the barbs return to place.
3. Closely examine the down feather with a hand lens. Locate the rachis, barbs, and barbules. Draw and label your observations in the space provided in Figure 3.
4. Notice the flexibility of the shaft of the down feather. Gently ruffle the down feather and then try to smooth it as you did the contour feather.
5. Repeat steps 1 and 2 with the feather taken as evidence by the British customs service.

Contour feather (magnified)	Down feather (magnified)	Feather taken as evidence (magnified)

Feather taken as evidence (additional observations)

FIGURE 3

6. Observe the shape, coloring, and other characteristics of the feather taken as evidence. Draw and label this feather in the space provided in Figure 3. Also, record whether this feather is a down or contour feather, along with any other observations that you made. Use the terms in Figures 1 and 2 in recording your observations to make your notes as precise as possible.

7. Compare your observations of the feather taken as evidence to the information given in Figure 2 and in the BioDetectives Background to determine whether this feather is one of the types shown in Figure 2.

ANALYSIS AND CONCLUSIONS

1. **Comparing and Contrasting** Is the feather taken as evidence by the British customs service a contour or down feather? What observations support your conclusion?

_____

_____

_____

_____

_____

_____

_____

2. **Analyzing Data** Were you able to identify the species of the feather taken as evidence? If so, what species is it?

_____

_____

_____

_____

_____

_____

_____

3. **Observing** What characteristics of the feather taken as evidence did you use to identify its source?

_____

_____

_____

_____

_____

_____

_____

_____

4. **Drawing Conclusions** Forensic scientists often begin identification of a feather by comparing it to those of the common domesticated birds shown in Figure 2. If a feather taken as evidence does not match any of these species, what would you recommend as a second step? Explain your answer.

_____

_____

_____

_____

_____

_____

_____

_____

_____

5. **Communicating Results** Write a report to the British customs service recommending whether to return the seized goods or to charge the owner with a crime. Be sure to include information from your observations to support your position.

_____

_____

_____

_____

_____

_____

_____

_____

_____

_____

_____

_____

_____

_____

_____

_____

_____

_____

_____

_____

_____

_____

_____

_____

_____

_____

_____

_____

_____

_____

Tracking a Plague

Background

Epidemiologists are scientists who study the causes of diseases and how they spread. When the number of cases of a disease suddenly increases, epidemiologists try to determine why this is happening. They also suggest ways to bring the disease under control. By interviewing patients, their families, and anyone the patients may have come in contact with, epidemiologists look for patterns in how people became ill. Epidemiologists also use laboratory tests to determine what may have caused the disease.

Many of the techniques that epidemiologists use are based on the work of John Snow, a British doctor who lived in the 1800s. At that time, millions of people lived in crowded, unsanitary cities. Diseases spread quickly in these areas, killing thousands. Anthrax, a bacterial disease, raged through herds of horses, cattle, sheep, and goats, infecting tannery workers and animal herders. In 1831 and 1832, cholera, another bacterial disease, broke out in London, England, killing 23,000 people. Disease outbreaks such as these that affect large numbers of people are called epidemics.

In the early 1800s, most people thought that diseases were caused by cold, damp air. But Snow believed that the cause of many diseases could be found in water. Snow first learned about cholera when he was an 18-year-old apprentice physician. He was sent to northern England to treat sick coal miners during a cholera outbreak. This experience caused Snow to make the prevention of such epidemics his lifelong goal. In the summer of 1854, while Snow was attending medical school in London, another cholera epidemic occurred there. At that time, the Thames River was the main source of drinking water in London. Snow suspected that there was a connection between the Thames River and the people who were getting sick. Because the disease affected the patients' intestines and not

their lungs, Snow thought that it was probably transmitted by drinking water.

In the 1800s, household waste was collected in pits located under people's houses. As the waste in these pits decomposed, it seeped out into the surrounding soil. The waste from those pits located near the Thames obviously made its way into the river. As the weather became warmer, cholera struck. This time it caused 250,000 cases and more than 50,000 deaths.

Snow was determined to find the source of this disease. He collected the addresses of nearly 2,700 people who were sick with cholera. Then, he marked these addresses on a map of London. Snow's map also showed the name of the company that provided water to each neighborhood. Because Snow suspected the river water, he counted the cases that occurred in houses served by each water company. He discovered that customers of the Southwark & Vauxhall Water Company were far more likely to have cholera than were people who obtained their water elsewhere. Snow investigated this company, and found that the water it sold came from a part of the Thames near a leaking waste pit. After he publicized his findings, the cholera epidemic started to decline as people began to avoid this contaminated source of water.

Just as the early summer cholera outbreak was fading, a new cluster of cases flared up in another area of London. This time, when Snow mapped the locations of the cases, he found them grouped together around a well on Broad Street, shown in Figure 1 on page 34. People who lived near wells pumped their own water and carried it home in buckets. Just like the Thames, the Broad Street well was contaminated with sewage containing cholera bacteria. The disease was spread as each bucket of water was drawn. Snow asked government officials to take the well out of service. They agreed and removed the pump handle so the well could not be used. Within a short period of time, the number of new cholera cases decreased dramatically.

Snow's success in helping to control a cholera epidemic shows how today's epidemiologists can affect public health. To this day, epidemiologists use many of Snow's methods, including interviews and case mapping, to search for clusters of cases as Snow did.

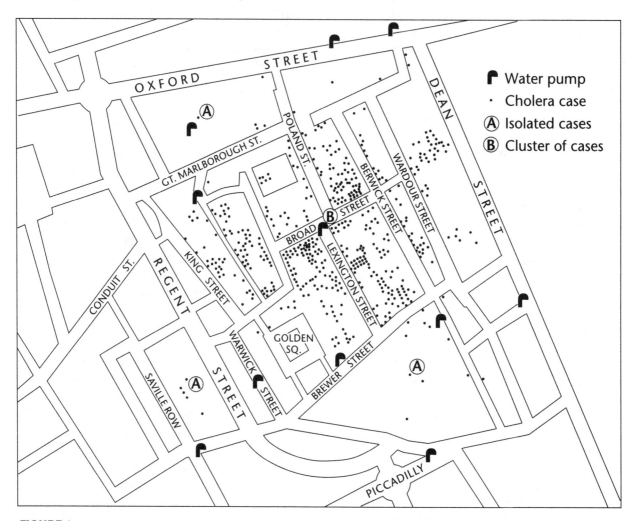

FIGURE 1

Tracking a Plague

Investigation

CASE SUMMARY

Imagine that doctors in the United States have begun to see a reappearance of cholera. Ninety-seven cases have been reported in eight cities between July 5 and July 25. Interviews with the patients have revealed that all of them ate oysters shortly before becoming ill. Officials suspect that these oysters were sold illegally without being inspected.

Public health doctors are interested in tracking the course of the disease to prevent any further cases. Law enforcement officials want to find out how the oysters were illegally imported and sold. You have been given data to analyze for clues explaining how the outbreak began and spread, and whether it is increasing or decreasing.

QUESTIONS FOR FORENSIC ANALYSIS

When and where did the oysters enter the country? How did they get to the cities where cholera occurred? Is the number of new cases of cholera increasing or decreasing?

MATERIALS (per group)

United States map
tracing paper

PROCEDURE

1. Use the map of the United States to locate the 8 cities listed in Figure 2.
2. Place the tracing paper over the map. Mark the location of each city on the tracing paper.
3. Next to the mark that indicates each city, write the dates of the outbreak and the number of cases that correspond to that location.

HYPOTHETICAL DISTRIBUTION OF CHOLERA CASES

City	Dates of Outbreak	Number of Cases
Houston, Texas	July 5–15	14
Louisville, Kentucky	July 10–20	8
Memphis, Tennessee	July 8–18	14
Minneapolis, Minnesota	July 13–23	4
New Orleans, Louisiana	July 6–16	13
Pittsburgh, Pennsylvania	July 15–25	2
St. Louis, Missouri	July 11–21	10
St. Petersburg, Florida	July 6–16	12

FIGURE 2

4. Look for patterns in the dates, number of cases, and the relative locations of the affected cities. On the lines below, record your observations of these patterns.

_____

_____

_____

_____

ANALYSIS AND CONCLUSIONS

1. **Using Tables and Graphs** List the cities in Figure 2 in the order in which the cases of cholera appeared.

_____

_____

2. **Comparing and Contrasting** Is the number of cases increasing or decreasing as the disease spreads? Explain how the data from two cities support your answer.

_____

_____

_____

3. **Predicting** Where might the next cases of cholera be reported? Explain your answer.

_____

_____

_____

4. **Formulating Hypotheses** Propose a hypothesis of how the cholera outbreak may have begun.

_____

_____

_____

5. **Drawing Conclusions** Based on the data, how do you think the disease traveled from city to city? Explain your answer.

_____

_____

_____

6. On a separate sheet of paper, write a short paragraph describing the history of this outbreak of cholera.

Name_____ Class_____ Date _____

Evaluating Pollen Evidence

Background

Because many plants produce pollen that is spread widely by wind, pollen is found in many environments. Most wind-borne pollen grains never arrive at a flower. Instead, they settle on various objects in the environment. The outer layers of a pollen grain are composed of tough materials that do not break down easily. As a result, pollen grains can still be found long after they have settled out of the air. In addition, the pollen grains of different plant species vary widely in size, shape, and surface features when seen under the microscope.

Forensic scientists often use pollen grains found in the dust on clothing and other physical evidence to determine where these objects have been. Many of the features that scientists use to identify pollen are related to how the pollen normally travels from the male to the female flower parts. For example, most wind-pollinated plants produce large numbers of small, light, threadlike pollen grains. Because this kind of pollen grain is so light, wind easily carries it over long distances. Wind-borne pollen from plants that grow in Africa has been found as far away as Florida.

Many plants depend on animals such as bees and bats to carry pollen from flower to flower. These plants make less pollen than those that depend on wind because the pollinating animals travel directly between flowers. Many animal-borne pollen grains are larger than wind-borne pollen grains. Animal-borne pollen grains are covered with spines and hooks that help attach them to the animals—surface features that can be used to identify the species of pollen grains.

By using a compound light microscope, forensic scientists can view the surface features of pollen grains. Although scientists who identify pollen

grains normally work with a magnification of 400 ×, the general features of pollen grains can usually be seen at a magnification of 100 ×. At this magnification the shape of the grain, its texture, and the locations of grooves and pores can be seen. To find pores, a scientist stains the pollen sample with iodine and lightly squeezes the sample between a microscope slide and a coverslip. This pressure forces a few of the starch granules stored in the pollen grain out through the pores in its surface. The stained pollen grain will appear slightly red, and the starch granules will become black. The starch granules are a good clue that the speck of dust that released them is a pollen grain. The location and number of pores also help the forensic scientist identify the species of the pollen.

To record what they have seen through the light microscope, scientists make sketches and notes. A forensic scientist sketches a pollen grain while looking into the microscope with one eye and focusing the other eye on a sheet of paper. The paper is placed close to the side of the microscope, at the same height as the microscope stage. An image of the pollen grain appears on the paper. The scientist can then directly trace the outline of the pollen grain with a pencil. The sketched image will be at about the same magnification as the image seen through the microscope.

The scientist sketches the pollen grain as seen from the side and from the end, recording its width and length. The location, number, and size of any pores, grooves, or spikes on the pollen grain are also recorded. Figure 1 on page 38 shows some notes and sketches that were made of pollen from a common southwestern species of tree, bigtooth maple (*Acer grandidentatum*). The pollen was viewed at a magnification of 500×. The scientist has drawn several pollen grains in Figure 1A; notice the views of a single pollen grain from the side in Figure 1B, and from the end in Figure 1C. The width and length of the pollen grains have also been recorded.

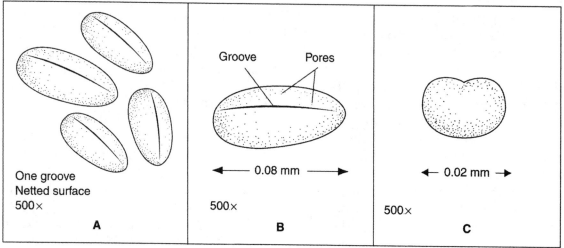

FIGURE 1

Evaluating Pollen Evidence

Investigation

CASE SUMMARY

The district attorney is preparing a criminal case for trial. In this case, police detectives collected dust samples from a suspect's home. The forensic laboratory found pollen grains in this dust that linked the suspect to the crime scene. In pre-trial hearings, the defense attorney has challenged this evidence, claiming that a dust sample taken from nearly any room would contain similar pollen grains. The district attorney has asked you to test this claim.

QUESTION FOR FORENSIC ANALYSIS

Can you find pollen grains in samples of dust from a randomly chosen room? If you do find pollen grains in the dust, are they identical to the pollen found in the evidence?

MATERIALS (*per group*)

microscope
2 textbooks
metric ruler
prepared slide of pollen found on the evidence
microscope slide
coverslip
plastic gloves
iodine solution
unlined white paper
dropper pipette

SAFETY

Iodine is poisonous and can stain skin and clothing. Do not get it in your mouth. Pollen and dust can cause allergic reactions. If you have asthma or allergies, do not perform steps 8 and 9. Glass coverslips and microscope slides can easily break and cut you.

PROCEDURE

1. Place the prepared slide of pollen found in the evidence on the stage of the microscope. View the slide at a magnification of 100 × and, if possible, at a higher magnification. Observe and compare the pollen grains on the slide.

2. Place a sheet of unlined paper on top of one or two textbooks so that it is close to the same height as the prepared slide. Place the books and paper on the same side of the microscope as your writing hand.

3. Choose a pollen grain that is turned so that you can see its entire length, as shown in Figure 1B. Examine the pollen grain through the microscope with your left eye if you are right-handed, or your right eye if you are left-handed. Be sure to keep both eyes open. The image of the pollen grain should appear on the unlined paper.

4. Sketch the pollen grain. Note the locations of any pores, grooves, or other surface features. If either your sketch or the pollen grain disappears, close the eye that is seeing the stronger image for a few seconds. The disappearing part will reappear.

5. Use a metric ruler to measure the length of the pollen grain in your drawing. Divide this measurement by the magnification of the microscope that you used to make the sketch. The result will be the approximate length of the pollen grain. Record this measurement on your sketch.

6. Move the slide until you locate another pollen grain that you can see from the end, like the one in Figure 1C. Using the procedure in Steps 2 through 4, sketch this view of the pollen grain.

7. Using the procedure in step 5, calculate the width of the widest part of the pollen grain. On your sketch, record this measurement. Record on your sketch the magnification, and any other observations you make concerning the appearance of the pollen grains.

8. Put on plastic gloves. Use a clean sheet of paper to scrape a sample of dust from an environmental surface in your classroom. **CAUTION:** *Do not perform steps 8 and 9 if you have allergies or asthma.* Fold the paper and let the dust fall into the fold. Pour the dust from the fold onto a clean microscope slide.

9. Use a dropper pipette to place one drop of iodine on the dust sample. **CAUTION:** *Iodine is poisonous. If any iodine gets on your skin, immediately rinse it off with cold water.*

10. Carefully place a coverslip over the dust sample and iodine drop. Fold a paper towel in half several times so that it is four or eight layers thick. Place the folded paper towel carefully over the coverslip to absorb any iodine that may seep out from between the coverslip and slide.

11. With the paper towel still in place on the coverslip, gently and carefully press down on the paper towel, coverslip, dust sample, and slide to squeeze starch granules out through the pores of any pollen grains present. **CAUTION:** *Coverslips can break and cut you.*

12. View this slide under a magnification of at least 100 ×. Look for pollen grains in the dust sample. To help identify any pollen grains present, pay particular attention to black masses of starch granules spilling out of pores in the pollen grains. Record your observations. If you find any pollen grains, repeat steps 2 through 7 to record detailed notes and sketches of each type of pollen that you observe.

13. Compare your observations with those of your classmates to determine whether many students observed pollen similar to that on the prepared slide.

ANALYSIS AND CONCLUSIONS

1. Observing Describe any pollen you observed in the dust sample you collected.

_____

_____

2. Comparing and Contrasting Compare the surface features of the pollen found in the evidence with those of any pollen you observed in the dust sample you collected. How are the two samples similar? How are they different?

_____

_____

_____

_____

3. Comparing and Contrasting Compare the size and shape of any pollen you observed in the dust sample you collected with the size and shape of the pollen found in the evidence.

_____

_____

4. Observing Describe any starch granules you saw on each slide. Did both samples contain pollen grains that released starch granules from similar patterns of pores?

_____

_____

_____

_____

5. Drawing Conclusions Did your observations support the defense attorney's claim that similar pollen can be found in the dust in any room? Explain your answer.

_____

_____

_____

_____

_____

_____

_____

_____

Interpreting Insect Evidence

Background

Forensic scientists often use insects and other arthropods as evidence in criminal cases when these animals are found in stolen or illegal goods. In these cases, insects can help identify the country or type of environment from which the goods were sent. A forensic scientist can also examine insects found in the grill and tire treads of a car to determine where the car has been.

Many insect species are found only in specific parts of the world. Forensic scientists can use these species as clues to the country or region from which evidence may have come. Other types of insects are found only in certain habitats. These insects provide information about the type of environment in which the evidence has been. For example, dragonflies live in water for up to three years before developing into flying adults. Because adult dragonflies must lay their eggs in water, these insects live near lakes, marshes, and other bodies of fresh water. Thus, a forensic scientist who finds a dragonfly in a stolen car can conclude that the car has been near water.

To use insects as clues, a forensic scientist must know how to identify the insects that are sent to the laboratory. Insects make up the class Insecta in the phylum Arthropoda. The class Insecta contains several orders. To determine in which order an insect belongs, a scientist must examine its body structure. Some important features to consider in classifying an insect are the structure of the head, including mouthparts, antennae, and eyes; the structure of the thorax and abdomen; and the number and kind of wings. Many insects with wings are often referred to as "flies" of one type or another; however, these insects actually can belong to many different orders.

The order Ephemeroptera, for example, consists of mayflies. Like dragonflies, these insects breed only near water. Finding a mayfly in a crate is evidence that the crate was near water at some time. Figure 1 lists some examples of insect orders that are found in specific types of environments.

Finding an insect such as a mayfly in evidence indicates only that it has been near water. To learn more about where that water is located, a forensic scientist can try to identify the insect's species. Different

**EXAMPLES OF INSECT ORDERS
FOUND IN SPECIFIC HABITATS**

Order of Insects	Common Name	Habitat
Odonata	Dragonflies, damselflies	Aquatic as larvae
Ephemeroptera	Mayflies	Aquatic as larvae
Mecoptera	Scorpionflies, hangingflies	Forests with dense ground cover
Trichoptera	Caddis flies	Aquatic as larvae
Siphonaptera	Fleas	Parasites on land mammals and birds
Isoptera	Termites	Dead trees and wooden structures

FIGURE 1

species within the same order have different ranges. If the insect happens to have only a small geographic range, the list of lakes and streams where the evidence might have been becomes much shorter.

In contrast to mayflies and dragonflies, some insect orders include species that live in many kinds of environments. For example, the order Coleoptera consists of the beetles. Some beetle species are found only in tropical deserts; others live in the forests of North America. Some beetles feed mostly on one type of crop. These specialized species are common only in or near fields of that crop. Finding a beetle in evidence is helpful only if the specific type of beetle can be identified. To help identify insects, forensic scientists use field guides, insect collections, and other reference materials.

Interpreting Insect Evidence

Investigation

CASE SUMMARY

Police detectives have confiscated a stolen art shipment. They found several insects within the crates where the art was hidden. They have asked you to help identify these insects. The detectives are hoping that this identification will give clues as to the source of the stolen art.

QUESTION FOR FORENSIC ANALYSIS

Where was the stolen art packed into the crates?

MATERIALS (per group)

4 preserved insects
dissecting microscope or hand lens
field guides to insects
4 different colored pencils
plastic gloves

PROCEDURE

1. Put on a lab apron and plastic gloves. Using a dissecting microscope or hand lens, observe the insect specimens from all sides. Note the number of wings and any special legs and mouthparts. Closely inspect each insect's head, thorax, and abdomen.

2. Use the dichotomous key in Figure 2 on page 46 to identify the order of each insect specimen. To use the dichotomous key, examine each specimen, and then read statement 1 (number of wings). Then, go to statement 1a. If the insect has wings, go to statement 2. If the insect has no wings, go to statement 3. Continue through the dichotomous key until you have identified the insect's order. Record the order of the insect specimen in the Data Table on page 47.

3. Repeat step 2 for each of the insects.

4. After you have recorded the order of each insect specimen, use a field guide to determine the species of each insect. Record the species and common name of each insect specimen in the Data Table.

5. Use a field guide to determine the geographic range of each insect species. On the map in Figure 3 on page 47, outline and label the geographic range of each insect species. Use a different color to show the range of each species.

6. Use the field guide and the information in Figure 1 to determine the habitat of each insect species. Record this information in the Data Table.

DICHOTOMOUS KEY TO SIX ORDERS OF INSECTS

	1. Number of wings 1a) Insect has no wings..go to 2 1b) Insect has two pairs of wings..go to 3
2a	**2.** Specialized body form 2a) Body flattened and vertical...................Order Siphonaptera (fleas) 2b) Body not flattened and vertical...go to 6
3a	**3.** Shape of wings 3a) Front wings triangular with many veins and much larger than hindwings.................Order Ephemeroptera (mayflies) 3b) Wings oval in shape...go to 4
4a	**4.** Hair on wings 4a) Wings covered with fine hair...........................Order Trichoptera (caddisflies) 4b) Wings not covered with fine hair...go to 5
5a	**5.** Shape of head 5a) Head elongated into a beak.............................Order Mecoptera (scorpionflies, hangingflies) 5b) Head not elongated into a beak...go to 6

6a
 	
6b
	6. Shape of body
	 6a) Body antlike in shape, but broad where
	     the abdomen joins the thorax.................................Order Isoptera (termites)
	 6b) Very long, thin thorax
	     and abdomen.................................Order Odonata (dragonflies, damselflies)

FIGURE 2

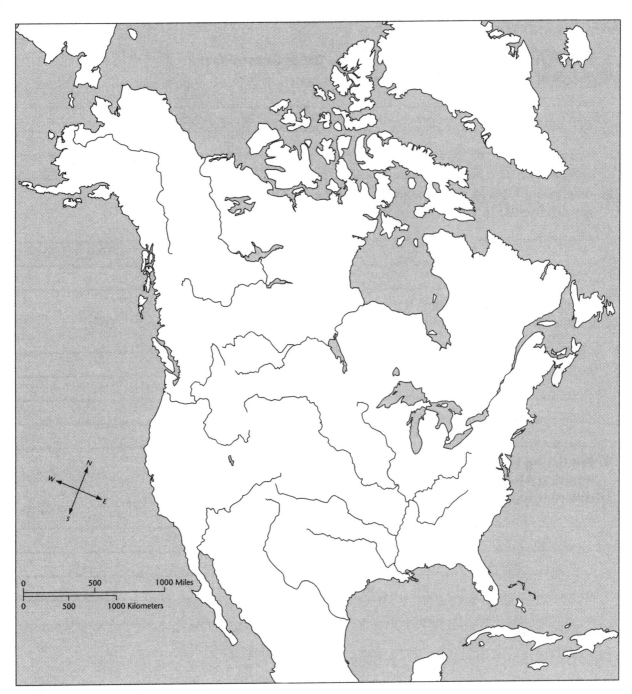

FIGURE 3

DATA TABLE

Specimen	Order	Species	Common Name	Habitat
1				
2				
3				
4				

ANALYSIS AND CONCLUSIONS

1. **Classifying** What characteristics did you use to determine the orders of the insect specimens?

_____

_____

_____

_____

2. **Analyzing Data** In what geographical area are all four insect species found? In what type of habitat do they live?

_____

_____

_____

3. **Communicating Results** What can you conclude about where the stolen art was packed into crates? Be as specific as possible.

_____

_____

_____

_____

_____

4. **Predicting** How might your map in step 5 and your answer to question 3 have been different if the specimens had consisted of different species of the same orders? Explain your answer.

_____

_____

_____

_____

_____

Interpreting Skeletal Remains

Background

Whenever skeletal remains of unknown or suspicious origin are discovered, forensic scientists are called upon to help identify the bones or solve the mystery. Bones that are carefully collected and examined can reveal a surprising amount of information.

The first task of the forensic scientist is to determine whether the bones are human. Human bones are easy to recognize. The human skull, for example, has a much larger braincase for its size than the skull of any other animal. The bones of the human leg provide yet another clue. The ends of these bones, which form the knee joint, are especially wide. The widened knee joint enables a person's weight to be spread over a large area, which reduces stress on the knees.

If the bones are found to be human, then the forensic scientist and the police carefully dig up the site where the bones were discovered. They perform this work slowly to discover evidence such as any fibers, hair, and insects. Another reason for their slow pace is that old bones may be fragile and must be handled gently.

After bringing the bones to the laboratory, the forensic scientist tries to determine whose bones they were. This task depends on the slow, careful collection of many small clues such as the shape of the skull and the roughness of joint surfaces. A skeleton also can reveal the person's approximate age, sex, and muscular build, and much about how the person lived and died. Some of the small bones in the fingers, for example, fuse as a child develops. A forensic scientist can estimate a child's age from the condition of these bones.

The teeth and bones of the skull also provide many clues to an individual's age and sex. An adult has 32 teeth, unless some have been lost. The third molars, or "wisdom teeth," do not emerge from the jaws until the late teens. This fact can help determine the age of a teenager or young adult. Wear and tear on the tooth surfaces provides another clue to the age of remains. The more worn the tooth surfaces, the older the person is thought to be.

The bones of the skull are especially useful for estimating age. These bones are partly separate at birth. Their edges gradually fuse from birth to age 50. The fused edges of these bones are called sutures. Figure 1 on page 50 shows the locations of some of the sutures of the skull. A forensic scientist can estimate the age of a skeleton by examining these sutures. All three sutures labeled in Figure 1 begin to close at about age 21. The suture at the rear of the skull, shown in Figure 1C, begins to close more quickly after age 26, and is fused by age 30. Figure 1C also shows how the left and right sides of the skull form a suture on top of the skull. This suture closes by age 31 or 32. The last suture to close runs across the top of the skull from side to side just above the forehead, as seen in Figures 1A and B. This suture is not fused until about age 50.

Figure 1 also shows some of the differences between male and female skulls. Males tend to have large, square chins, whereas females have smaller, rounded chins. Females have a sharp border around the eye socket, and males have pronounced eyebrow ridges.

Changes in the pelvis, or hipbone, and other bones provide clues to the age of a skeleton. One such clue that indicates adulthood is the fusion of the parts of the pelvis into a single bone. As adults age, their bones lose calcium, causing pits and rough areas to form in the surfaces of smaller bones and the ends of long bones. At the same time, the smooth, distinct edges of young bones become irregular and shaggy.

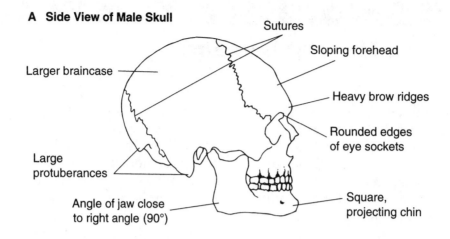

A Side View of Male Skull

Sutures

Sloping forehead

Larger braincase

Heavy brow ridges

Rounded edges of eye sockets

Large protuberances

Angle of jaw close to right angle (90°)

Square, projecting chin

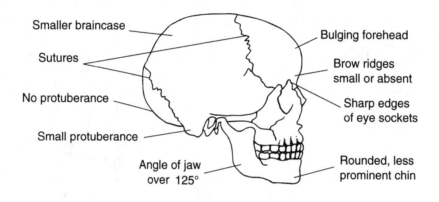

B Side View of Female Skull

Smaller braincase

Bulging forehead

Sutures

Brow ridges small or absent

No protuberance

Sharp edges of eye sockets

Small protuberance

Angle of jaw over 125°

Rounded, less prominent chin

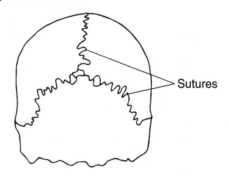

C Posterior (Rear) View of Skull

Sutures

FIGURE 1

In addition to the fact that the skeleton of a male is usually larger and heavier than that of a female, the pelvis also can be used to determine a person's sex. In females the pelvis is thinner and less dense than it is in males. Notice in Figure 2 on page 51 that the male pelvis is deep and funnel-shaped, with a narrow angle in front (50°–80°). The female pelvis is shallow and broad, and forms a wider angle (90°–100°). The wider, more open female pelvis allows for the passage of a baby during childbirth.

The sacrum is the part of the spine that attaches to the pelvis. The sacrum is straight in females and slanted inward in males. The coccyx, or "tailbone," curves inward below the pelvis in males, but is nearly straight and vertical in females.

Name_____ Class _____ Date _____

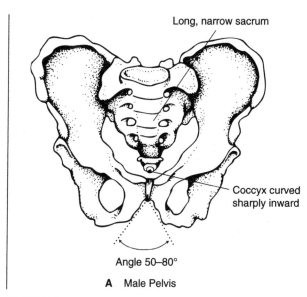

Long, narrow sacrum

Coccyx curved sharply inward

Angle 50–80°

A Male Pelvis

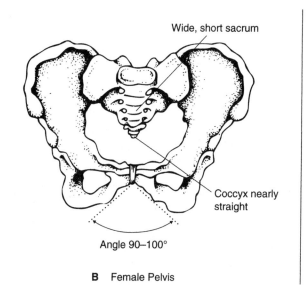

Wide, short sacrum

Coccyx nearly straight

Angle 90–100°

B Female Pelvis

FIGURE 2

If a femur, or thighbone, is the only bone that a forensic scientist has to examine, it is possible to determine the individual's height and muscular build. Forensic scientists use a simple equation to estimate the person's height from the length of the femur. Forensic scientists also know that stouter bones are necessary to support heavier frames. Thus, a femur that is thick compared to its length indicates that the person was relatively heavy. Because exercise strengthens the point where the muscle is attached to the bone, a large mark where the muscle was attached is a sign that the person was muscular. Larger muscle-attachment scars on the bones of one arm as compared to the other indicate whether the person was right- or left-handed. Frequent, repeated stress on a joint can wear down the cartilage of the joint, causing the joint surface to appear smooth and shiny. If this kind of wear is found in the right shoulder joint, for example, the person may have spent a lot of time carrying heavy objects on the right side, as a postal worker or plumber might do.

Teeth and bones can also provide clues to a person's medical history. For example, a prolonged fever in childhood can temporarily stop tooth development, leaving a telltale ring on the teeth. Spaces between teeth, crowns, fillings, or other dental work make each person's teeth unique. Once the identity of the skeleton has been narrowed to a small number of possibilities, the teeth can be compared to dental records to settle the question. Bones can provide other medical information. They may be weakened by osteoporosis, a common disease of older adults in which the loss of calcium makes the bones fragile. A scar on a bone is a sign of a healed fracture.

The skeleton can even reveal a person's personal habits and diet. A flattening of the surfaces of the molars, for example, may mean that the person tended to grind his or her back teeth. Eating certain foods on a regular basis, such as hard candies or high fiber plant materials, can wear down the surfaces of specific teeth.

Interpreting Skeletal Remains

Investigation

CASE SUMMARY

While digging a foundation for a new building, construction workers found some buried bones that appeared to be human. Thinking they were being helpful, the construction workers placed the bones into a box and took them to the nearest police station. The police identified the bones as human and have asked you to examine the bones and to provide as much information as possible about them.

QUESTION FOR FORENSIC ANALYSIS

What can you determine about the person whose bones were found by examining the bones?

MATERIALS (*per group*)

preserved or plastic skeleton or individual bones

anatomical charts of the human skeleton

metric ruler

protractor

calculator (optional)

PROCEDURE

1. Using anatomical charts, identify each bone. Examine the bones carefully and note any damage, scars, or other special characteristics of the bones and teeth. On the lines below, record whether the skeleton is complete and note any special characteristics that you observe. If the skeleton is not complete, list the name of each bone examined.

   _____

   _____

   _____

   _____

   _____

   _____

   _____

   _____

2. Examine the sutures of the skull to see how much fusion has taken place. Count the teeth to determine whether a full set of 32 adult teeth is present. Note any signs of damage to the teeth. Observe whether the surfaces of the bones, the ends of the long bones, and the edges of the pelvis are smooth or rough. Record your observations on the lines below.

_____

_____

_____

_____

_____

_____

3. Using Figures 1 and 2 as guides, examine the skull and pelvis for male and female characteristics. Use a protractor to measure the angle of the pelvis, which is labeled in Figure 2. Note the shape of the sacrum and whether the coccyx curves inward. Record your observations on the lines below.

_____

_____

_____

_____

4. If a femur is present, measure the length of this bone in centimeters. Record this measurement on the line provided.

Femur length: _____ cm

Then, use the following equation to estimate the individual's approximate height.

$$\text{Height (cm)} = (2.26 \times \text{femur length}) + 66.38$$

(This equation is accurate to within 3.4 cm.)

Record the person's estimated height below.

Estimated height: _____ cm

5. On a separate sheet of paper, construct a Data Table to organize the observations you made in steps 1 through 4. Record all your observations in your data table.

ANALYSIS AND CONCLUSIONS

1. **Inferring** How might the construction workers have been more helpful to you as a forensic scientist?

_____

_____

_____

2. **Analyzing Data** Which bones were most useful in identifying the remains?

_____

_____

3. **Communicating Results** Write a report describing the person whose bones you examined. Include as much information as possible.

_____

_____

_____

_____

_____

_____

_____

_____

_____

_____

_____

_____

4. **Evaluating** Which of your conclusions about the person whose bones you examined were simple and clear-cut? Which conclusions were more difficult to make?

_____

_____

5. **Drawing Conclusions** How does your answer to question 4 help explain why courts are sometimes skeptical about this kind of forensic evidence?

_____

_____

_____

Identifying Blood

Background

In the investigation of some criminal cases, the police collect evidence that includes bloodstains. Forensic scientists are often asked to identify these stains, a task that involves a series of separate tests. Because stains from other substances such as rust, paint, and fruit juice often look like blood, the first test is done to confirm that the stain is blood. If the stain is found to be blood, the next step is to find out whether the blood is human. Finally, a test to determine the specific human blood type is performed.

Two kinds of tests can be used by a forensic scientist to test the stain for the presence of blood. One kind of test uses a chemical that reacts with an enzyme in blood to produce a deep pink color or a glowing light. The other kind of test involves a chemical that forms a crystal when blood is present.

If the forensic scientist determines that the stain is blood, the scientist then uses proteins called antibodies to find out whether the blood is human. Antibodies are defensive proteins produced by animals. These proteins bind to any foreign substance such as a virus that enters an animal's body. The antibodies "mark" the foreign substance for destruction by special white blood cells that the animal produces. The forensic scientist treats the bloodstain with antibodies from a rabbit that bind to human proteins. If these antibodies bind to the blood in the stain, the blood is human.

The last test determines the blood type of the stain. To understand blood types, you first need to know what blood is. Blood is a tissue that consists of several kinds of cells

floating in a straw-colored fluid called plasma. The two main kinds of cells in blood are red blood cells and white blood cells. Red blood cells are more numerous than white blood cells and carry oxygen throughout the body. White blood cells attack foreign substances or organisms. In addition to water, dissolved gases, salts, nutrients, enzymes, hormones, waste products, and several types of plasma proteins, plasma contains antibodies.

Red blood cells have a surface coating of carbohydrate molecules, which can be of three kinds. The simplest kind of carbohydrate coating on red blood cells produces blood type O. Two other blood types, called type A and type B, contain red blood cells covered by more complex carbohydrate molecules. Some blood cells carry both type A and B carbohydrate molecules, producing blood type AB.

A forensic scientist can determine the blood type of a blood sample by treating it with antibodies called anti-A and anti-B. Anti-A binds to type A carbohydrate molecules and anti-B binds to type B carbohydrate molecules. When either of these antibodies binds to red blood cells, they form visible clumps. Figure 1 on page 58 shows that the red blood cells in both blood type A and type AB carry type A carbohydrate. Therefore, if a blood sample clumps after being treated with anti-A, the sample must be either blood type A or blood type AB. If the sample clumps after being treated with anti-B, then the blood must be type B or type AB. Neither antibody causes blood type O to clump.

Blood Type	Carbohydrates on Red Blood Cells	Reaction to Anti-A	Reaction to Anti-B
A	A	Clumping	No clumping
B	B	No clumping	Clumping
AB	A and B	Clumping	Clumping
O	Neither A nor B	No clumping	No clumping

FIGURE 1

By comparing the blood type in a bloodstain to a suspect's blood type, a forensic scientist can determine whether the blood may have come from the suspect. However, this blood-type test cannot prove that the blood in the stain came from a certain person. Because there are only four possible blood types in this particular system (A, B, AB, and O), many people share the same blood type. In the United States, 43% of the population have blood type O, 42% have blood type A, 12% have blood type B, and 3% have blood type AB. Thus, blood type evidence can only prove that a bloodstain did not come from a certain person.

For positive identification, a different test, such as a DNA fingerprint, must be performed. One method of using DNA to identify a person is explained in Investigation 1 of this book. Although DNA-based tests can identify individuals more precisely than blood-type tests can, many forensic laboratories still perform a blood-type test before analyzing the DNA in a bloodstain. Then, if more information is needed, the forensic scientists can try to extract DNA from the bloodstain for analysis.

Identifying Blood

Investigation

CASE SUMMARY

A family arrived at their home to find that it had been burglarized. They called the police, who investigated the area and discovered a broken window. The police officers also found red stains on the broken glass, on a curtain in front of the broken window, and on the carpet below the window. Suspecting that the burglar might have been injured while breaking the window, the police officers brought the stained curtain to the forensic laboratory for analysis. The police also collected blood samples from a suspect and from the two family members who live in the house. You have been asked to determine whether the stain is blood and, if the stain is blood, to find out whether it is the suspect's blood or a family member's blood.

QUESTION FOR FORENSIC ANALYSIS

Is the red stain blood? If it is blood, is it the same type as the blood of the suspect or of either of the family members who live in the house?

MATERIALS (per group)

laboratory apron   plastic gloves
safety goggles   microscope slide
cloth with red stain   dropper pipette
3 simulated blood samples (from suspect   coverslips
    and 2 family members)   compound microscope
scissors   simulated blood-typing kit
forceps

SAFETY

Put on a laboratory apron and safety goggles before starting this activity. Use caution with sharp instruments such as scissors and with glass microscope slides and coverslips that can break and cut you. Put on plastic gloves before Step 3.

PROCEDURE

1. To determine whether the stain is blood, use scissors to cut a small sample of the stained area from the cloth. Using the forceps, place the sample on a microscope slide so that it lies flat. Use a dropper pipette to place a drop of water on the sample. Add a coverslip.

2. View the cloth with the microscope at low and high magnification. Look for any clues that indicate whether the stain on the cloth is blood. Record your observations as a labeled drawing and notes in the space provided below.

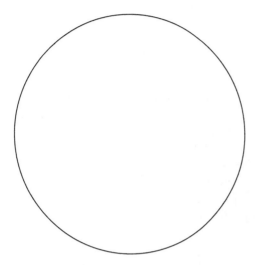

3. Put on the plastic gloves. Use the anti-A and anti-B antibody solutions in the simulated blood-typing kit to test the stained cloth and each blood sample. The procedure for this test depends on the kind of simulated blood-typing kit that you are using. Your teacher will provide instructions for the use of your kit. After you add an antibody solution to the sample, the antibody may react with the sample by forming a clump. Record the results of each test in the Data Table.

DATA TABLE

Sample	Reaction to Anti-A	Reaction to Anti-B

ANALYSIS AND CONCLUSIONS

1. **Analyzing Data** Was the stain blood? Explain how your observations support your answer.

   _____

   _____

   _____

   _____

   _____

   _____

2. **Evaluating** Why was it necessary to test both the suspect's blood and the family members' blood?

   _____

   _____

   _____

3. **Analyzing Data** Which types of red-blood-cell carbohydrates—A, B, or O—are present in the bloodstain? Explain your answer.

   _____

   _____

   _____

4. **Drawing Conclusions** Based on the results of the blood-type tests, whose blood could be on the curtain? Explain your answer.

   _____

   _____

   _____

   _____

5. **Evaluating** What can you conclude from your observations about the suspect's involvement in the burglary? Explain your answer.

   _____

   _____

   _____

   _____

   _____

Unit 1 History's Mystery: An Introduction to Forensic Science

1. The scientists used a thermometer, plaster casts, cameras, adhesive tape, microscopes, DNA analysis equipment, and chromatography apparatus. **2.** The scientists observed matches between the bootprint and John Toms' boot; between the DNA on his sleeve and the victim's DNA; between the fibers found under the victim's fingernails and in Toms' vest; and between the traces of gunpowder on Toms' face and on the victim.

Unit 2 *Pfiesteria*: A Killer in the Water

1. Dr. Burkholder hypothesized that *Pfiesteria* was causing the disease. **2.** The organism was difficult to identify because it can change form to the point that it is not recognizable, and the harmful forms can disappear quickly after a fish kill.

Unit 3 Skin Cancer: Deadly Cells

1. A vaccine was used to stimulate the production of large numbers of lymphocytes that would attack the cancer cells. **2.** The scientists made observations, formed a hypothesis based on those observations, and tested their hypothesis by experiment.

Unit 4 Coming Home: A Nation's Pledge

1. Scientists surveyed the area to identify likely sites, sifted through soil, examined and photographed all remains collected, compared their observations to medical records, and performed mitochondrial DNA analysis. **2.** Mitochondrial DNA in the remains was compared to the mitochondrial DNA of missing soldiers' maternal relatives.

Unit 5 The Galápagos Islands: A Glimpse Into the Past

1. Darwin's observations of the organisms there, including the finches, helped him to formulate his theory of evolution. **2.** Dr. Stedman hypothesized that the lava tubes held fossils that could reveal the evolutionary history of the Galápagos, including ancient, extinct species. He tested his hypothesis by digging in the lava tubes to find fossils.

Unit 5 Mummies: Ties to the Past

1. The scientists made physical observations and performed chemical analyses of the skeletons and teeth. **2.** The scientists made inferences about diet and activities based on the chemical composition and physical condition of the skeletons and teeth.

Unit 6 Hantavirus: A Tale of Mice and People

1. The scientists tested the victims' blood against hundreds of toxic and infectious agents and found that a virus was responsible. Then, they tested the victims' blood against many known viruses and used the victims' blood to induce symptoms in animals that were found to resemble hantavirus. **2.** The scientists hypothesized that the disease was caused by hantavirus and spread by contact with rodents. **3.** The scientists concluded that people are infected by contact with the virus in mouse droppings.

Unit 8 Insect Clues: The Smallest Witnesses

1. The variables in Dr. Bass' experiments included the ages and species of insects, rate of decomposition, time, and temperature. **2.** Knowledge of the life cycle of flesh-decomposing insects enabled scientists to determine the age of remains from the species of insects on a body and their stage of development.

Unit 9 Wrongly Accused: Science and Justice

1. The forensic expert should have done preliminary research to determine how specific the characteristics of hair are to an individual, and should have included controls and more samples from other people in the comparison of hairs. **2.** The scientists compared DNA from the suspect with that collected at the crime scene and showed that they did not match.

Unit 10 Influenza: Tracking a Virus

1. One hypothesis was that the virus was an avian (bird) strain that infected humans; a second hypothesis was that the virus was a swine strain. The second hypothesis was found to be correct. **2.** The scientists were able to use differences in DNA sequence between avian and swine influenza viruses to identify the origin of the virus.

Investigation 1
Using Polarized Light
to Identify Fibers

ADVANCE PREPARATION

To make a set of fiber samples for the class, affix a tuft of fibers from each of the sources listed below to one end of a two-inch piece of transparent tape. Label each appropriately on a scrap of paper attached to the other end of the tape as follows:

- *3 samples of the same kind of carpet fiber.* Label one as a reference sample of carpet from the victim's home; the next, as an unknown found in the victim's home, and the last, as an unknown found in the suspect's home.
- *2 samples of human hair from the same person.* Label one as a reference sample of the victim's hair; the other, as an unknown found in the suspect's home.
- *2 samples of cat or dog hair.* Label one as a reference sample of hair from the victim's pet, the other, as an unknown from the scene of the crime.

Using a microscope slide as a template, cut out pieces of polarizing film to fit under the students' microscope slides. Be sure to cut all pieces in the same orientation so that their planes of polarization will be the same.

To make each analyzer, drill a 1/2-inch hole in the center of the bottom of a 35-mm film canister. Using a nickel or a quarter as a template, cut a circular piece of polarizing film. Glue the polarizing film into the inside of the film canister so that it covers the hole you drilled. Make a copy of Figure T-1 for each analyzer. Cut out each copy of Figure T-1 and remove the center of each copy, leaving a paper ring.

Hold one of the slide-shaped polarizing filters you made earlier vertically. Hold the film canister in front of the slide-shaped filter so that you are looking at a bright light through both filters.

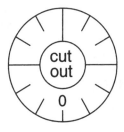

Template for paper ring for analyzers. Photocopy and cut out a copy of this ring for each analyzer.

FIGURE T-1

Rotate the film canister until the image is darkest. Use white correction fluid to mark the side of the film canister that is now at the 9 o'clock or 3 o'clock position. Place the film canister upside down on the table. Glue the paper ring onto the bottom of the film canister with the zero on the paper ring aligned with the white mark on the film canister.

The analyzers can be reused.

SAFETY

While wearing plastic gloves, clean all fiber samples with detergent and water before use by students. **DO NOT EXPOSE STUDENTS TO DOG OR CAT HAIRS IF THEY HAVE ALLERGIES TO THESE ANIMALS.** Students should use caution with dissecting probes and glass microscope slides and coverslips.

TEACHING STRATEGIES

- Demonstrate the effect of rotating one polarized filter with respect to a second. This demonstration can be done on an overhead projector. Show students that light transmission varies from brightest to darkest over 90 degrees of rotation.
- Use a large copy of Figure T-1 (on the chalkboard or overhead projector) to show students how to read the index marks at 30-degree intervals on the analyzer. Explain that they will be recording angles of rotation relative to the position of the analyzer in Step 5, with the zero in the 6 o'clock position.

ANALYSIS AND CONCLUSIONS

1. Answers will depend on materials provided, but they should be based on specific similarities among samples in shape, texture, and behavior in polarized light. **2.** Answers will depend on the samples provided, but students should see clear differences among carpet fibers, animal hairs, and human hairs. **3.** The evidence may indicate that the suspect was at the crime scene or that the victim was in the suspect's home at some time, but it cannot prove that the suspect committed the crime. **4.** Answers should briefly summarize a reasonable conclusion and provide specific, convincing evidence to justify this conclusion. For example, when fibers found in the suspect's home and at the crime scene were examined through the microscope with polarized light, they appeared similar to the victim's hair, carpet fibers, and pet's hair. These similarities suggest that the suspect and the victim came into contact.

Investigation 2
Using Range and Habitat to Track Evidence

SAFETY

You might want to display examples of different fungi in the classroom. Before bringing any fungi into the classroom, make certain that no students who may be exposed to the fungi have allergies or asthma.

TEACHING STRATEGIES

If possible, gather recent news articles on the local use of forensic mycology for students to read.

ANALYSIS AND CONCLUSIONS

1. All the species found occur either in Australia or in the coastal areas of Borneo or Sumatra. **2.** The shipment was packed somewhere on the coast of Borneo or Sumatra. **3.** The cookies were made or packed with the diamonds in a wooded area near a stream and termite nests. **4.** Spores of Australian fungi probably fell into the package while it was being inspected in Australia. **5.** No, it is too dry in the Sahara Desert to allow most fungi to grow.

Investigation 3
Using Tissues as Evidence

ADVANCE PREPARATION

Obtain prepared slides of normal and cancerous human lung tissue from a biological supply company. The prepared slide of the "patient's" lung tissue consists of a slide of cancerous tissue with its label covered.

You may choose to refer students to Figure 37–18 in *Prentice Hall Biology*, which is a photograph of lung sections from a smoker and a nonsmoker.

SAFETY

Instruct the students in safe handling of the microscope and glass slides.

TEACHING STRATEGIES

- Begin the investigation by distributing and discussing news articles about evidence issues in tobacco-related lawsuits.
- Culminate the investigation by distributing and discussing news articles about the judgments in lawsuits by cancer victims and their families against tobacco companies.

ANALYSIS AND CONCLUSIONS

1. Students should observe uniformly fine, spongy alveolar tissues in the normal lung, and dark deposits, larger open spaces, and solid tumor tissue in the cancerous lung. **2.** Answers will depend on materials provided. Students may observe the large spaces and tough fibrous tissue typical of emphysema. **3.** The patient's lung tissue should share with the cancerous lung tissue the characteristics described in question 1. **4.** Students should express confidence in the diagnosis of smoking-induced cancer in the patient. The similarity of the patient's tissue to the cancerous tissue and its difference from the healthy tissue should be clear. **5.** The solid tumor mass reduces the surface area available for gas exchange. This makes it more difficult for the patient to obtain oxygen.

Investigation 4
Interpreting DNA Analysis

ADVANCE PREPARATION

Students should read Chapters 12 and 13 in *Prentice Hall Biology* before performing this investigation. Give students two copies of page 23, so they can keep one copy as part of the Background reading and return the other as part of the investigation.

TEACHING STRATEGIES

- Discuss the concept of enzymes as tools. Point out that, just as a hand tool is an instrument used to manipulate a mechanical device without becoming a part of the device, enzymes are chemical instruments that control the rates of chemical reactions without being changed by the reaction.
- To help students understand the amplification rate of PCR, use Figure 2 to explain that each PCR cycle doubles the number of DNA molecules. Then, ask students to determine the results of repeated doublings by calculating the values of powers of 2: 2^1, 2^2, 2^3, and so on. You may choose to have them use a calculator to determine exactly how many amplified DNA strands would result from 20 PCR cycles that operated with perfect efficiency: $2^{20} = 1,048,576$.

ANALYSIS AND CONCLUSIONS

1. The samples in lanes B, E, and F contained DNA molecules that were approximately 1 kilobase long. Lanes C, E, and F contained DNA molecules that were approximately 2 kilobases long. **2.** These samples provided standards for estimating the lengths of the DNA molecules in the other lanes. **3.** The 3.5 and 4 kilobase bands represent DNA sequences that are present in all the samples. They give no information for differentiating one sample from another. **4.** Samples from the crime scene and from the suspect's shoe included all the components of both the victim's and the suspect's amplified DNA. It is reasonable to conclude that the suspect was present at the scene of the crime. (The evidence does not demonstrate that the suspect is guilty of the crime.)

Investigation 5
Identifying Feathers

ADVANCE PREPARATION

Obtain feathers from a biological supply company or a local source such as a zoo, poultry-packing plant, or pet store. If the feathers have not already been sterilized, put on plastic gloves and wash the feathers gently in a warm, soapy bath of 10% bleach solution. Then, rinse and dry the feathers before giving them to students. Down feathers can also be found in pillows. Some examples of domestic birds that can be used for samples are dove, rooster, pheasant, pigeon, turkey, crow, and chicken.

SAFETY

Because feathers may contain parasites and pathogenic organisms, it is important to wash them before use. If you are gathering the feathers yourself, wear plastic gloves for protection while handling them.

TEACHING STRATEGIES

- You might choose to introduce the investigation with an introduction to endangered species and why they are protected. The importance of biodiversity to humans and the natural world should be stressed.
- To further identify feathers, you may want to make flash cards out of bird field guides, magazines, or other sources.

ANALYSIS AND CONCLUSIONS

1. Answers will depend on the type of feather you provide, but students should cite evidence such as the interlocked barbules and thick rachis of contour feathers, and the short, flexible rachis and unattached barbules of down feathers. **2.** Answers will depend on the type of feather provided. **3.** Answers should include specific details about the coloring, structure, and shape of the feather. **4.** Students should mention using additional library and Internet resources, including those from the U.S. Fish and Wildlife Service to compare the feather to those of other birds

until it has been identified. **5.** Students' paragraphs should cite characteristics of the evidence feather that were important in its identification, such as coloring, structure, and shape.

Investigation 6
Tracking a Plague

ADVANCE PREPARATION

Provide each student or small group with a United States map showing major cities and rivers, along with a sheet of tracing paper as large as the map.

ANALYSIS AND CONCLUSIONS

1. Houston, New Orleans, St. Petersburg, Memphis, Louisville, St. Louis, Minneapolis, Pittsburgh. **2.** The incidence decreased as the disease spread northward. Evidence can be found by comparing the number of cases in any of the Gulf coast cities with those in Pittsburgh and Minneapolis. **3.** Any city upstream of Minneapolis on the Mississippi or upstream of Pittsburgh on either the Monongahela or Allegheny rivers could be a logical candidate for the next cases. **4.** Possible student response: The cholera bacteria originated in the Gulf of Mexico and entered the human population when uninspected oysters were illegally brought to Gulf coast cities. **5.** The cholera bacteria were spread by distribution of contaminated oysters up the Mississippi River as far as Minneapolis and up the Ohio River to Pittsburgh. **6.** Student responses should note that the outbreak began in cities on or near the Gulf coast and spread inland and northward as it declined in severity.

Investigation 7
Evaluating Pollen Evidence

ADVANCE PREPARATION

Prepared pollen slides are available from biological supply houses, but most are not stained with iodine. You or your students can also prepare your own permanent mounts of pollen that you collect and stain with iodine.

Either Lugol's iodine solution or tincture of iodine sold as a disinfectant will work as a stain.

SAFETY

Carefully supervise student preparation of dust sample slides. Iodine is poisonous. Students should use caution with glass microscope slides and coverslips, which can break and cut hands. Students with dust or pollen allergies should not work with or near dust samples.

TEACHING STRATEGIES

- After introducing the investigation, make sure students can sketch directly from the microscope.
- Review with students how to measure the width of the field of view of the microscope and how to use this information to estimate the sizes of objects they observe.
- Discuss the importance of the distance of the drawing paper from students' eyes. If time permits, suggest that they try holding the paper closer than the microscope stage and then farther away while they sketch the same image at each distance. Ask them to compare the size of the figure in each sketch. The farther away the paper is held from the eye, the larger the sketched figure will be.
- You can put a blank Data Table on the chalkboard or overhead projector to facilitate data sharing among students (step 13).

ANALYSIS AND CONCLUSIONS

1. Answers will depend on student observations. If students observed pollen, answers should include a description of the size, shape, and surface features of the pollen. **2.** Answers may include descriptions and comparisons of surface features such as pits, pores, spikes, grooves, or hooks. **3.** Most pollen grains are approximately 0.02 to 0.1 mm wide and slightly longer. **4.** If students observed pollen in their dust samples, answers should include the observation that black, iodine-stained starch granules were expelled from pores in the pollen grains when the slide was squeezed. Commercially prepared slides of pollen are usually not stained with iodine or pressed to force out starch granules. **5.** Answers should be supported by references to the students' observations.

Investigation 8
Interpreting Insect Evidence

ADVANCE PREPARATION

Provide each student or small group with four specimens of common insects of the orders listed in Figure 1. Label the specimens 1 through 4. Select species that are easily identified with the field guides provided to students. There should be at least some area where the ranges of all these species overlap. Order preserved specimens from a biological supply company or provide specimens of local species.

TEACHING STRATEGIES

- This activity is easily adaptable to whatever specimens you have available. Most supply companies offer several species within each order, so you may wish to provide each group with specimens of different species.
- This activity can be set up at a series of stations, or with different groups being assigned specimens from either aquatic or terrestrial habitats.

ANALYSIS AND CONCLUSIONS

1. Number, shape, and structure of the wings; shapes of body segments **2.** Answers will depend on species used, and should be consistent with students' maps (Figure 3). **3.** Acceptable answers will reflect the range and habitat of the insects provided. **4.** Other species in these orders live in the same types of habitats, but some are found in other geographic areas. Therefore, students' conclusions of where the art was packed into crates might be different.

Investigation 9
Interpreting Skeletal Remains

TEACHING STRATEGIES

- You may choose to prepare a mock burial of a whole skeleton to introduce the setting as a crime scene.
- If an entire skeleton is unavailable, students can perform this investigation with a femur, pelvis, and skull or with diagrams and/or written descriptions.
- You may need to show students how to use the protractor or to help them identify some parts of the skull.
- Students may need help in designing their Data Tables.

ANALYSIS AND CONCLUSIONS

1. The construction workers would have been more helpful if they had called the police immediately upon discovery of the bones instead of removing the evidence from the scene. **2.** The skull, pelvis, and femur are most useful. **3.** Answers should include a description that includes sex and approximate age and height. Additional conclusions may be possible, depending on the materials provided. **4.** Determination of sex and height is not difficult, but students may recognize that precise determination of age is more difficult. **5.** Because some characteristics, such as age, can be difficult to determine from skeletal remains, the courts sometimes do not rely on the conclusions of forensic science.

Investigation 10
Identifying Blood

ADVANCE PREPARATION

Simulated blood-typing kits are available from scientific supply houses.

Cut a small piece of cloth for each lab group to represent the curtain taken by the police. Place a drop of type A "blood" from the simulated blood-typing kit on each piece of cloth and let dry. Label the vials of simulated blood types A, AB, and O as "Suspect," "Family Member 1," and "Family Member 2," respectively.

SAFETY

Be sure the students carry the microscope safely with two hands and are careful to avoid breaking the glass slides.

TEACHING STRATEGIES

- This investigation does not deal with the genetics of blood type. However, you may choose to review the genetic aspects by referring students to Figure 14-4 and the accompanying explanation of the ABO blood-group system in Section 14-1 of *Prentice Hall Biology*.
- If you are using this investigation with several classes, change the blood types of the samples between classes. Word of the results may spread quickly among students.

ANALYSIS AND CONCLUSIONS

1. Yes, the presence of blood cells seen with the microscope supports this conclusion. **2.** This was done to determine whether the blood could have come from someone who lived in the house. **3.** Type A carbohydrates are present in the bloodstain, because the stain reacted only with anti-A antibody. **4.** The suspect's blood could be on the curtain because the blood types of the bloodstain on the cloth and the suspect's blood are the same. The family members have blood types AB and O, so the bloodstain could not have come from one of them. **5.** The results of the experiment indicate that the suspect could have been the burglar. However, the results do not prove that the suspect was involved, because 42% of Americans have blood type A.